in times of

illness

Praise for *In Times of Illness*

Robert Hamma has woven together a tapestry of prayer that covers us, protects us, and warms us during illness. This book gently guides us into the spiritual updrafts of prayer that lead us to the healing energy God has planted in us. Regardless of our brokenness in body, in mind, or in spirit, this book not only offers consolation, it promises spiritual animation for our healing.

—**Richard P. Johnson, Ph.D.**
Association for Lifelong Adult Ministry

Praise for the *In Times of . . .* series

Life has hard times and the hardest sometimes is when we have to help ourselves or others through hard times. Where are we to get the insight, the resources to encourage and strengthen us? Where can we find the biblical passages to read and meditate by ourselves or with others? How can we express ourselves in faith when we are fearful, angry, exhausted, or doubtful?

Robert Hamma has the answer. In three brief, helpful books of ten sections each he gives us psalms, canticles, gospel passages, and his own meditations that comfort, cheer, and inspire us in time of need.

—**William G. Storey, D.M.S.**
author of *Lord Hear Our Prayer*

A simple, consoling collection of prayers for those who are sick, grieving, or giving care to others. It will be a wonderful help for people in times of stress and distress, particularly helping them to pray in and through their real lives and intense emotions. I recommend it as a healing resource for every Christian community.

—**Fr. Stephen Rossetti**
St. Luke Institute

PRAYERS OF HOPE & STRENGTH

in times of
illness

Robert M. Hamma

ave maria press AMP Notre Dame, Indiana

---

www.avemariapress.com

International Standard Book Number: 1-59471-029-5

Cover and text design by John Carson

Printed and bound in the United States of America.

Library of Congress Cataloging-in-Publication Data
Hamma, Robert M.
  In times of illness : prayers of hope and strength / Robert M. Hamma.
    p. cm.
  Includes index.
  ISBN 1-59471-029-5 (pbk.)
  1. Sick--Prayer-books and devotions--English. I. Title.

  BV270.H36 2004
  242'.86--dc22

                         2004006151

Contents

Introduction

Times of illness challenge us on many levels. We often feel physically, psychologically, and spiritually drained. Under such circumstances, prayer can be especially difficult.

It is hard to focus our minds when we are sick and words elude us. Lack of sleep and the side effects of medications may make us drowsy. And the pains in our bodies are a constant distraction. A host of conflicting emotions boil up within us; fear, anger, frustration, regret cannot simply be ignored or pushed below the surface. And on a spiritual level, the feeling of comfort or the assurance of faith that we seek may seem like just a faint memory.

At times like this it is helpful to remember two things. The first is that the desire to pray is itself a prayer. We would not long for God, we would not want to pray, if God had not already put that desire in our hearts. The fact that you are reading or hearing these words is a sign God has placed a desire to pray within you.

No matter how weak or infrequent that desire may be, it is a grace of the Spirit. No matter if you have not prayed in years and feel guilty about turning to God now that things are falling apart, the recognition that you need God is itself an invitation from God to come home. No matter what hurt, what harm, what sin you may have committed, the desire for peace of heart is the beginning of God's work in you.

The second thing to remember is summed up in this traditional bit of wisdom: Pray as you can, not as you can't. There is no right or wrong way to pray. For some, the prayers of childhood may return; for others, the familiar practices of a lifetime may be best. Our prayer may last but a second, or we may toss and turn through the night, calling out to God with every breath. Structure may be helpful to some, while others will want to make it up as they go along.

Both the desire to pray and our feeble attempts at prayer are the work of the Holy Spirit within us. As St. Paul said in the Letter to the Romans: "The Spirit helps us in our weakness; for we do not know how to pray as we ought, but that very Spirit intercedes with sighs too deep for words" (8:26). Sometimes the very best prayers are the simplest. Did not Jesus hear the prayers of these people in the gospels who called out to him:

Lord, that I may see.
Lord, that I may hear.
Lord, that I may walk.
If you will, you can heal me.

The best way, indeed the only way to pray is from our hearts. If we do that, any prayer we make is a true and genuine prayer of faith.

Using This Book

This book is written simply to help you pray. While it has a certain structure and format, feel free to use it as you wish. Hopefully the format of psalms, scripture, prayers, and meditations will make it easy and flexible to use.

In Times Of Illness is organized into ten chapters. Each of these chapters focuses on particular feelings that we often experience during sickness. These emotions, whether positive, such as trust or gratitude, or negative, such as loneliness or fear, can be very helpful starting points for prayer. If prayer is an expression of the heart, then the feelings in our hearts are a good place to begin. A brief introduction to each chapter helps bring the dimensions of each experience to the surface and invites us to turn to God in the midst of those experiences.

Within each of these chapters, there are two sections. The first is called "A Brief Time of Prayer." The structure of this part is as follows:

Psalm
Reading
Breath Prayer
Closing Prayer

A psalm has been chosen that expresses the particular feeling or disposition within us at this particular moment. A brief line, traditionally called an antiphon, expresses the theme of the psalm and is normally recited before and after the psalm is prayed. Then a "psalm prayer" reiterates the theme of the psalm in light of the experience of illness. Next, a brief gospel reading speaks to us about what we are going through. It helps us identify with a moment in the life of Jesus or one of his followers when they too experienced something like what we are experiencing here and now.

A brief time of reflection after the reading is helpful if one is able, otherwise move directly to the next part, a one-line prayer called a "breath prayer." This prayer is modeled on the ancient practice of the Jesus Prayer, which is repeated meditatively in rhythm with one's breathing: "Lord Jesus Christ, Son of the living God, have mercy on me, a sinner." The breath prayers in each chapter can also be easily prayed with the rhythm of our breathing. For example, the breath prayer during times of pain is "Do not fear, for I am with you." The first phrase, "Do not fear," can be spoken inwardly as you breathe in, and the second, "for I am with you," can be prayed as you breathe out. This process can be repeated for as long as you wish. It can be used throughout the day or in the lonely hours of the night.

The brief time of prayer ends with a closing prayer, either the Lord's Prayer or one of the biblical canticles found in the Everyday Prayers section of the book. While the brief time of prayer can be used at any time of day, the concluding canticles are taken from the church's morning, evening, and night prayer and may be selected accordingly.

Each brief time of prayer can be prayed alone or with another. One way to use this book is as a resource for a caregiver, a family member, or a friend to pray with someone who is ill. Perhaps you could also use it when a pastoral minister visits you at home, in the hospital, or in some other care facility. The prayers and readings in the second part of each chapter may also be used in the context of these brief times of prayer.

The second section of each chapter offers prayers and readings that can be used as the need arises. The prayers are taken from a variety of classic and contemporary sources. Those not attributed to another source have been composed by the author. There are two additional readings, one from scripture and another from a spiritual writer whose reflections offer insight and consolation during these times.

Prayer reminds us that we are not alone as we go through hard times. Whether our loved ones are present to offer us comfort and support or at a distance, prayer reminds us that we are not alone. The words of the psalms, prayers, and readings place us in touch with Christians throughout the world and of previous generations who have used these very words to find courage and strength in times of need. And the Lord, our shepherd and our friend, is with us always.

I pray that this book will be a source of comfort and healing for you during this difficult time.

Everyday Prayers

Morning Prayer

Loving God, as morning breaks,
I offer you praise for the gift of life.
I pray for the wisdom and strength
   of your Holy Spirit
so that I may be ready for whatever this day
   will bring.
Teach me to see Christ in everyone with whom I
   have contact today—
whether family or friends, doctors or nurses,
caregivers or others who are ill.
Grant me patience in pain,
the compassion to look beyond myself,
and trust to believe you are with me.
You are my strength, O Lord, I rely on you
   this day.

Evening Prayer

As daylight fades, and night approaches,
I long for you, O Lord.
You have been with me through this day,
stay near me now as darkness falls.
Sustain my hope and do not let my trust weaken.
Show your mercy and compassion
to me and to all who suffer.
You are my light, O Lord, when darkness
    surrounds me.

Night Prayer

Heavenly Father, as this day ends,
I give you thanks for the quiet ways your love
    has been with me.
Grant me peaceful sleep
and let your healing Spirit be at work in me
to restore me to health and to help me
    grow in trust.
I ask this in the name of Jesus, the Lord. Amen.

During a Sleepless Night

Lord, I cannot sleep. I lie awake, thinking about
  things and worrying.
I worry about my health, my family, the future—
  a countless number of things.
I am weary but I find no rest.
I remember your words:
"Can any of you by worrying add a single hour to
  your span of life?" (Mt 6:27).
Help me to take your words to heart, O Lord.
Let me place each concern in your hands.
Grant me peace, O Lord, and let me sleep.

Canticle of Zachary

This biblical song is traditionally prayed as part of the church's morning prayer.

Blessed be the Lord, the God of Israel;
he has come to his people and set them free.
He has raised up for us a mighty Savior,
born of the house of his servant David.

Through his holy prophets he promised of old
that he would save us from our enemies,
from the hands of all who hate us.
He promised to show mercy to our ancestors
and to remember his holy covenant.

This was the oath he swore to our
    father Abraham:
to set us free from the hands of our enemies,
free to worship him without fear,
holy and righteous in his sight
all the days of our life.

You, my child, shall be called the prophet of the
Most High;
for you will go before the Lord to prepare
his way,

to give his people knowledge of salvation
by the forgiveness of their sins.

In the tender compassion of our God
the dawn from on high shall break upon us,
to shine on those who dwell in darkness and the
    shadow of death,
and to guide our feet on the way to peace.

Glory be to the Father, and to the Son
    and to the Holy Spirit:
as it was in the beginning, is now,
    and will be forever. Amen.

Canticle of Mary

This biblical song is traditionally prayed as part of the church's evening prayer.

My soul proclaims the greatness of the Lord,
my spirit rejoices in God, my Savior;
for he has looked with favor on his lowly servant.

From this day all generations will call me blessed:
for the Almighty has done great things for me,
and holy is his Name.

He has mercy on those who fear him
in every generation.

He has shown the strength of his arm,
he has scattered the proud in their conceit.

He has cast down the mighty from their thrones,
and has lifted up the lowly.

He has filled the hungry with good things,
and the rich he has sent away empty.

He has come to the help of his servant Israel
for he has remembered his promise of mercy,
the promise he made to our ancestors,
to Abraham and his children for ever.

Glory be to the Father, and to the Son
    and to the Holy Spirit:
as it was in the beginning, is now,
    and will be forever. Amen.

Canticle of Simeon

This biblical song is traditionally prayed as part of the church's night prayer.

Lord, now let your servant go in peace;
your word has been fulfilled:

my own eyes have seen the salvation
which you have prepared in the sight of
   every people;
a light to reveal you to the nations
and the glory of your people Israel.

Glory be to the Father, and to the Son
   and to the Holy Spirit:
as it was in the beginning, is now,
   and will be forever. Amen.

Chapter 1

When You Are in Pain

There are many kinds of pain that we experience in times of illness. We may be in physical pain, emotional pain, or spiritual pain. Often we experience all three, though in different degrees at different times. There is a sense of helplessness when we are in pain, sometimes even a sense of desperation. We long for relief, waiting impatiently for the next medication, the next visitor, the next moment of grace.

Many of us have been taught to be tough in times of pain, not to express our feelings. But there is nothing wrong with asking for help when we need it. Sharing our pain with another can offer some relief and enable others to do what they can for us.

Jesus certainly experienced physical, emotional, and spiritual pain. He allowed Simon of Cyrene to help him carry his cross and the women along the way to comfort him. And he cried out in prayer to his Father. Let us join our pain to his and find relief in him.

❧ A Brief Time of Prayer ❧

Psalm 42

Antiphon: The steadfast love of the Lord is always with me.

As a deer longs for flowing streams,
so my soul longs for you, O God.
My soul thirsts for God, for the living God.
When shall I come and behold the face of God?
My tears have been my food day and night,
while people say to me continually,
"Where is your God?"

These things I remember, as I pour out my soul:
how I went with the throng,
and led them in procession to the house of God,
with glad shouts and songs of thanksgiving,
a multitude keeping festival.
Why are you cast down, O my soul,
and why are you disquieted within me?
Hope in God; for I shall again praise him,
my help and my God.

My soul is cast down within me;
therefore I remember you
from the land of Jordan and of Hermon,
    from Mount Mizar.
Deep calls to deep at the thunder of your
    cataracts;
all your waves and your billows have gone
    over me.
By day the LORD commands his steadfast love,
and at night his song is with me,
a prayer to the God of my life.

I say to God, my rock, "Why have you
    forgotten me?
Why must I walk about mournfully
because the enemy oppresses me?"
As with a deadly wound in my body,
my adversaries taunt me,
while they say to me continually, "Where is
    your God?"

Why are you cast down, O my soul,
and why are you disquieted within me?
Hope in God; for I shall again praise him,
my help and my God.

Repeat Antiphon

Psalm Prayer

Lord Jesus Christ, you know well what it is like to be in pain and to suffer. Be with me now in the midst of this pain. Through the long hours of the night and in each moment of the day, let your love soothe me like the waters of a gentle stream. My soul is indeed cast down, yet I hope in you, my savior and my God.

Reading

Mark 15:16–24 *In our pain, we share in the sufferings of Christ.*

Then the soldiers led him into the courtyard of the palace (that is, the governor's headquarters); and they called together the whole cohort. And they clothed him in a purple cloak; and after twisting some thorns into a crown, they put it on him. And they began saluting him, "Hail, King of the Jews!" They struck his head with a reed, spat upon him, and knelt down in homage to him. After mocking him, they stripped him of the purple cloak and put his own clothes on him. Then they led him out to crucify him. They compelled a passer-by, who was coming in from the country, to carry his cross; it was Simon of Cyrene, the father of Alexander and Rufus. Then they brought Jesus to the place called Golgotha (which means the place of a skull). And they offered him wine mixed with myrrh; but he did not take it. And they crucified him, and divided his clothes among them, casting lots to decide what each should take.

Breath Prayer

Repeat this prayer in rhythm with your breathing for as long as you wish.

Do not fear, for I am with you.

Closing Prayer

Pray the Our Father or one of the Canticles in the Everyday Prayers section of the book.

✲ Prayers for Coping With Pain ✲

You Know What Pain Is Like

Lord Jesus,
you know what pain is like.
You know the torture of the scourge
   upon your back,
the sting of the thorns upon your brow,
the agony of the nails in your hands.
You know what I'm going through just now.
Help me to bear my pain
gallantly, cheerfully, and patiently.
And help me to remember that I will
   never be tried
beyond what I am able to bear,
and that you are with me,
even in this valley of the deep dark shadow.
In every pang that rends the heart,
the man of sorrows had a part;
He sympathizes with our grief
and to the suff'rer sends relief.
   —William Barclay

When Lord?

When will it end?
  When will it go away?
    When will I be at peace?
      When will I feel better?

The minutes are like hours and the hours are
  like days.
  How long have I to suffer?
    How long do I have to wait?

If I could see the end it would be easier to hope,
  to trust, to bear.
  If I knew that it is all planned out,
    I could accept it more easily.

But I don't know. I just wait and wait and wait.
  Please help me. Lord, let me feel you here, now
    with me and me with you.
Let me just live each moment.
  Help me to offer you each moment.
    No matter how many moments.
    —John Mueller

Prayer for Endurance

When I am weak,
  be with me, O God.
When pain gnaws at me,
  be with me, O God.
During dark moments,
  be with me, O God.
In lonely hours,
  be with me, O God.
If I get afraid,
  be with me, O God.
For patience with others,
  be with me, O God.
When I feel abandoned,
  be with me, O God.
To get me through this,
  be with me, O God.
  —Anonymous

❧ Readings for Times of Pain ❧

The Cup of Suffering *Jesus asks us, as he asked his disciples, "Can you drink the cup that I must drink?"*

Drinking the cup of life makes our own everything we are living. It is saying, "This is my life," but also, "I want this to be my life." Drinking the cup of life is fully appropriating and internalizing our unique existence, with all its sorrows and joys.

It is not easy to do this. For a long time we might not feel capable of accepting our own life; we might keep fighting for a better or at least different life. Often a deep protest against our "fate" rises in us. . . . We wish we were in another body, lived in another time, or had another mind! A cry can come out of our depths, "Why do I have to be this person? I didn't ask for it, and I don't want it."

But as we gradually come to befriend our own reality, to look with compassion on our own sorrows and joys, as we are able to discover the unique potential of our own way of being in the world, we can move beyond our protest, put the cup of our life to our lips and drink it, slowly, carefully, but fully.

—Henri Nouwen

Philippians 3:8–12 *We unite our pain with the suffering of Christ.*

More than that, I regard everything as loss because of the surpassing value of knowing Christ Jesus my Lord. For his sake I have suffered the loss of all things, and I regard them as rubbish, in order that I may gain Christ and be found in him, not having a righteousness of my own that comes from the law, but one that comes through faith in Christ, the righteousness from God based on faith. I want to know Christ and the power of his resurrection and the sharing of his sufferings by becoming like him in his death, if somehow I may attain the resurrection from the dead. Not that I have already obtained this or have already reached the goal; but I press on to make it my own, because Christ Jesus has made me his own.

Chapter 2

When You Get Bad News

Bad news. First there is the disbelief. "This can't be. There must be some mistake." Then there is the shock of it, the struggle to admit that this is really happening. Then, as it begins to take hold, there is the sense that your worst fears are coming true, the sense that this changes everything. Try as we might, we can't get away from it, it's always there.

What good are words at times like this? We don't know what to say, except to cry out in anger or fear. And so we should. But because our human words fail us, we turn to the word of God. And we turn to Jesus, who has walked this path before us, and to our brothers and sisters in faith, who have found strength in him in the midst of the darkness.

❧ A Brief Time of Prayer ❧

Psalm 31:1–5, 9–10, 14–16, 24

Antiphon: Be strong and let your heart take courage.

In you, O LORD, I seek refuge;
do not let me ever be put to shame;
in your righteousness deliver me.
Incline your ear to me; rescue me speedily.
Be a rock of refuge for me,
a strong fortress to save me.

You are indeed my rock and my fortress;
for your name's sake lead me and guide me,
take me out of the net that is hidden for me,
for you are my refuge.
Into your hand I commit my spirit;
you have redeemed me, O LORD, faithful God.

Be gracious to me, O LORD, for I am in distress;
my eye wastes away from grief,
my soul and body also.
For my life is spent with sorrow,
and my years with sighing;

my strength fails because of my misery,
and my bones waste away.

But I trust in you, O LORD;
I say, "You are my God."
My times are in your hand;
deliver me from the hand of my enemies
    and persecutors.

Let your face shine upon your servant;
save me in your steadfast love.
Be strong, and let your heart take courage,
all you who wait for the LORD.

Repeat Antiphon

Psalm Prayer

O Lord, hear my prayer, and in your compassion
rescue me. My heart is troubled and my thoughts
are confused. Do not leave me alone, for I place
my trust in you. Be gracious to me, O Lord, for I
am in distress.

Reading

Luke 8:41–42, 49–56 *Jesus is not swayed by bad news.*

Just then there came a man named Jairus, a leader of the synagogue. He fell at Jesus' feet and begged him to come to his house, for he had an only daughter, about twelve years old, who was dying. . . . [Then] someone came from the leader's house to say, "Your daughter is dead; do not trouble the teacher any longer." When Jesus heard this, he replied, "Do not fear. Only believe, and she will be saved." When he came to the house, he did not allow anyone to enter with him, except Peter, John, and James, and the child's father and mother. They were all weeping and wailing for her; but he said, "Do not weep; for she is not dead but sleeping." And they laughed at him, knowing that she was dead. But he took her by the hand and called out, "Child, get up!" Her spirit returned, and she got up at once. Then he directed them to give her something to eat. Her parents were astounded; but he ordered them to tell no one what had happened.

Breath Prayer

Repeat this prayer in rhythm with your breathing for as long as you wish.

My life is in your hands.

Closing Prayer

Pray the Our Father or one of the Canticles in the Everyday Prayers section of the book.

❧ Prayers for Coping With Bad News ❧

Why Lord?

WHY?
  Why now?
    Why this way?
      Why me?

I don't understand, Lord.
  I want to make sense out of the whole thing.
Is it something I did? Something I did wrong
  Is it somebody's fault?
  I want to blame somebody—You, them, myself.
It's not fair.
It's not fair—and I'm afraid and I'm angry
  and I'm confused.

Please help me. Please be with me.
  Please tell me it's going to be okay no matter
  what happens.
    Please.
    —John Mueller

The Power of Cancer

The power of cancer is very limited.
Cancer can liberate me from sudden death,
and give me time to prepare.
Cancer can rob me of a few years,
but cannot steal the joy of my life.
Cancer can attack my body,
but cannot snatch me
from the arms of my eternal father.
Cancer cannot damage friendship
nor wipe out memories.
Cancer cannot crush my faith,
nor separate me from the love of Christ.
Love conquers cancer.
    —Gregory Smutko, O.F.M. Cap.

Where There Is Pain

Where there is pain,
    God is present.
Where there is despair,
    hope is hidden.
Where there is oppression,
    freedom will rise.

Where there is hurt,
   healing waits.
Where there is conflict,
   peace shall again be born.
Where there is death,
   new life can grow.
If only we have eyes,
   that can see in the dark.
      —John D. Powers

O Living Christ

O living Christ, make me conscious of your
healing nearness;
Open my eyes that I may see you,
touch my ears that I may hear your voice,
enter my heart that I may know your love,
overshadow my soul and my body with your
presence that I may be still,
and that I may partake of your strength,
and your love,
and your healing life. Amen.
      —Russell B. Dicks

✒ Readings When You Hear Bad News ✒

Why Me? *There are so many questions in our minds. Only by allowing ourselves to ask these questions can we arrive at a deeper truth.*

Some people once brought a blind man to Jesus and asked him, "Rabbi, who sinned, this man or his parents that he was born blind?" They all wanted to know why this terrible curse had fallen on this man. And Jesus answered, "It was not that this man sinned, or his parents, but that the works of God might be made manifest in him." He told them not to look for why the suffering came, but to listen for what the suffering could teach them. Jesus taught that our pain is not punishment, it's no one's fault. When we seek to blame, we distract ourselves from an exquisite opportunity to pay attention, to see even in this pain a place of grace, a moment of spiritual promise and healing.
  —Wayne Muller

Matthew 14:10–13 *When confronted with the horrible news of John the Baptist's execution, Jesus withdrew from the crowds to pray.*

Herod had John beheaded in the prison. . . . John's disciples came and took the body and buried it; then they went and told Jesus. Now when Jesus heard this, he withdrew from there in a boat to a deserted place by himself.

Chapter 3

When You Are Afraid

Fear can wound us so terribly. It paralyzes us, leaving us uncertain of what to do or when to do it. It isolates us, preventing us from reaching out to loved ones and to God. It weakens us, robbing us of self-confidence and inner resolve.

But ultimately, fear has only as much power as we allow it to have. For as bad as the situation may be, we are not helpless, and certainly we are not hopeless. Perhaps we have the care and support of others to sustain us. Certainly we have the love of God to carry us. Whether we fear what we know or what we don't know, let us place ourselves in God's hands, God who promises to be with us no matter what may come.

❧ A Brief Time of Prayer ❧

Psalm 91

Antiphon: Do not be afraid, for I am with you always.

You who live in the shelter of the Most High,
who abide in the shadow of the Almighty,
will say to the LORD, "My refuge and my fortress;
my God, in whom I trust."

For he will deliver you from the snare of
   the fowler
and from the deadly pestilence;
he will cover you with his pinions,
and under his wings you will find refuge;
his faithfulness is a shield and buckler.

You will not fear the terror of the night,
or the arrow that flies by day,
or the pestilence that stalks in darkness,
or the destruction that wastes at noonday.

A thousand may fall at your side,
ten thousand at your right hand,
but it will not come near you.

Because you have made the LORD your refuge,
the Most High your dwelling place,
no evil shall befall you,
no scourge come near your tent.

For he will command his angels concerning you
to guard you in all your ways.
On their hands they will bear you up,
so that you will not dash your foot against
    a stone.

You will tread on the lion and the adder,
the young lion and the serpent you will trample
    under foot.
Those who love me, I will deliver;
I will protect those who know my name.

When they call to me, I will answer them;
I will be with them in trouble,
I will rescue them and honor them.
With long life I will satisfy them,
and show them my salvation.

Repeat Antiphon

Psalm Prayer

Draw me close to you, O Lord. Protect me in the shelter of your wings. For I am frightened and upset, afraid of what may come, both for me and those I love. Do not let this fear overwhelm me, but keep me focused on you and your presence. You are my refuge and my dwelling place, O Lord.

Reading

Matthew 14:22–33 *Reach out to Jesus in the midst of your fears.*

Immediately he made the disciples get into the boat and go on ahead to the other side, while he dismissed the crowds. And after he had dismissed the crowds, he went up the mountain by himself to pray. When evening came, he was there alone, but by this time the boat, battered by the waves, was far from the land, for the wind was against them.

And early in the morning he came walking toward them on the sea. But when the disciples saw him walking on the sea, they were terrified, saying, "It is a ghost!" And they cried out in fear. But immediately Jesus spoke to them and said, "Take heart, it is I; do not be afraid."

Peter answered him, "Lord, if it is you, command me to come to you on the water." He said,

"Come." So Peter got out of the boat, started walking on the water, and came toward Jesus. But when he noticed the strong wind, he became frightened, and beginning to sink, he cried out, "Lord, save me!" Jesus immediately reached out his hand and caught him, saying to him, "You of little faith, why did you doubt?" When they got into the boat, the wind ceased. And those in the boat worshiped him, saying, "Truly you are the Son of God."

Breath Prayer

Repeat this prayer in rhythm with your breathing for as long as you wish.

Take heart, I am here.

Closing Prayer

Pray the Our Father or one of the Canticles in the Everyday Prayers section of the book.

❧ Prayers for Coping With Fear ❦

How Lord?

How do I deal with all of this, Lord?
What are your expectations? What are mine?
What are others'?
Do I have to fake things? Do I have to hide
   my feelings?
   Do you want me to pretend that nothing is
      bothering me?
      Do you want me to act brave? What is brave?
I don't know what I am supposed to do.
   Do I let go? Do I fight like crazy? Can I cry?
      Can I be angry? I don't want to be angry
         with you.

I just don't know how I should be with you,
   with others.
   Help me Lord. Free me Lord.
      Help me to be just me—as I am—right now.
Help me not have to take care of everybody else.
   Free me Lord, just to be me.
      —John Mueller

Be, Lord

Be, Lord,
Within me to strengthen me,
without me to guard me,
over me to shelter me,
beneath me to stabilize me,
before me to guide me,
after me to forward me,
round about me to secure me.
—Lancelot Andrews

Litany in Time of Fear

From the fear of pain, deliver me.
From the fear of loss, deliver me.
From the fear of the unknown, deliver me.
From the fear of being powerless, deliver me.

When I am alone and afraid, be near me.
When I awake in the night, be near me.
When terror pursues me, be near me.
When I am losing hope, be near me.

Lord have mercy. . . . Lord have mercy.
Christ have mercy. . . . Christ have mercy.
Lord have mercy. . . . Lord have mercy.

Admitting Our Fear

Lord, I am afraid.
I don't like to admit it.
It seems that by admitting it,
I give more power to the fear,
more room for it to grow within me.

But I cannot hide from this fear.
It is always there.
Ignoring it does no good.
It catches me unaware,
and quickly overcomes me.

So listen to me, Lord.
When I say I am afraid,
I don't know how to resist this fear.
I give up my last defense
and cast myself upon you.

Only you can sustain me.

❧ Readings for Times of Fear ☙

Fear Not *Let us, like Jesus, learn to trust in the Father's love. This is what true faith, true religion, teaches us.*

The maxim of illusory religion runs: "Fear not, trust in God and he will see that none of the things you fear will happen to you"; that of real religion, on the contrary, is: "Fear not; the things you are afraid of are quite likely to happen to you, but they are nothing to be afraid of."
—William Barry, S.J.

Isaiah 43:1–5 *No matter what may befall us, God is always with us. God's love never leaves us.*

But now thus says the Lord, he who created you, O Jacob, he who formed you, O Israel: Do not fear, for I have redeemed you; I have called you by name, you are mine. When you pass through the waters, I will be with you; and through the rivers, they shall not overwhelm you; when you walk through fire you shall not be burned, and the flame shall not consume you. For I am the Lord your God, the Holy One of Israel, your Savior. I give Egypt as your ransom, Ethiopia and Seba in exchange for you. Because you are precious in my sight, and honored, and I love you, I give people in return for you, nations in exchange for your life. Do not fear, for I am with you. . . .

Chapter 4

When You Are Angry

Anger is a natural and normal response to sickness. The more sick we are, or the longer the illness lasts, the more likely we are to become angry. For some, anger is easily recognized and readily expressed. For others, anger is a difficult emotion to name, and it takes time to recognize it. Either way, we need to come to terms with our anger and recognize why we feel the way we do. Acknowledging our anger enables us to take the next step toward healing and peace.

Bringing this difficult emotion to prayer can help us take a step back from our struggle. It's okay to express our anger to God. There's a long tradition in the Bible of faithful people who let God know just how angry they were. Remembering that Jesus got angry sometimes, at his disciples as well as his adversaries, can give us some added perspective on this confusing emotion.

✺ A Brief Time of Prayer ✺

Psalm 13

Antiphon: How long, O Lord, will you forget me?

How long, O LORD? Will you forget me forever?
How long will you hide your face from me?
How long must I bear pain in my soul,
and have sorrow in my heart all day long?
How long shall my enemy be exalted over me?

Consider and answer me, O LORD my God!
Give light to my eyes, or I will sleep the sleep
  of death,
and my enemy will say, "I have prevailed":
my foes will rejoice because I am shaken.

But I trusted in your steadfast love;
my heart shall rejoice in your salvation.
I will sing to the LORD,
because he has dealt bountifully with me.

Repeat Antiphon

Psalm Prayer

Faithful God, hear my prayer. My soul is troubled, my heart swirls with anger like a raging sea. Do not abandon me as I cry out to you. Do not forget me. Give me the peace of your presence, now and always. Amen.

Reading

Luke 8:22–25 *Our anger is like a storm.*

One day he got into a boat with his disciples, and he said to them, "Let us go across to the other side of the lake." So they put out, and while they were sailing he fell asleep. A windstorm swept down on the lake, and the boat was filling with water, and they were in danger. They went to him and woke him up, shouting, "Master, Master, we are perishing!" And he woke up and rebuked the wind and the raging waves; they ceased, and there was a calm. He said to them, "Where is your faith?" They were afraid and amazed, and said to one another, "Who then is this, that he commands even the winds and the water, and they obey him?"

Breath Prayer

Repeat this prayer in rhythm with your breathing for as long as you wish.

Grant me your peace.

Closing Prayer

Pray the Our Father or one of the Canticles in the Everyday Prayers section of the book.

❧ Prayers for Coping With Anger ❧

Litany In Time of Anger

Jesus my Lord . . . be with me.
Jesus my Savior . . . be with me.
Jesus my Friend . . . be with me.

Word made flesh . . . be with me.
Living Water . . .
Healing touch . . .

Like me in all things but sin . . .
You know my frustration . . .
You too felt anger . . .

You rebuked Peter . . .
You challenged the Pharisees . . .
You cleansed the Temple . . .

When I call to you . . .
When I forget you . . .
Even if I turn away . . .

When I feel my chest tighten . . .
When my blood rises . . .
When I want to lash out . . .

When I want to hurt another . . .
When I am resentful . . .
When I have been wronged . . .

When I am afraid . . .
When I am fed up . . .
When I am angry . . .

Lord, have mercy.
Christ, have mercy.
Lord, have mercy.

Do Not Abandon Me

Sometimes Lord, I just want to scream . . . at the doctor, at the nurse, at my family . . . at you. I am just so angry about what has happened to me, about the way it's changed everything, about the way it's changed me.

My life has been thrown into chaos and I don't know where it is going. My body has betrayed me and it feels like you have too. Yet still, even in my anger, I call to you. Do not abandon me, for then I would be really lost. Stay by my side and be my strength.

Troubled by Anger

Merciful God, you made me in your image
and you know my every feeling.
You know how angry I am
and how hard it is for me to deal with that.
Help me to find ways to unburden my heart
without hurting others.
Help me to express my feelings to those
    whom I trust.
Do not let anger possess me,
or rob me of your presence.
Show me the way to peace and trust.

❧ Readings for Times of Anger ❧

Where Is God? *God's silence often compounds our anger.*

When you are happy, so happy that you have no sense of needing him, so happy that you are tempted to feel his claims upon you as an interruption, if you remember yourself and turn to him with gratitude and praise, you will be—or so it feels—welcomed with open arms.

But go to him when your need is desperate, when all other help is in vain, and what do you find? A door slammed in your face, and a sound of bolting and double-bolting on the inside. After that, silence. You may as well turn away. The longer you wait, the more emphatic the silence will become. There are no lights in the windows. It might as well be an empty house. Was it ever inhabited? It seemed so once. And that seeming was as strong as this.

What can this mean? Why is he so present a commander in our time of prosperity and so very absent a help in time of trouble?

—C. S. Lewis

Romans 8:31–35, 37–39 *Let nothing separate us from God.*

What then are we to say about these things? If God is for us, who is against us? He who did not withhold his own Son, but gave him up for all of us, will he not with him also give us everything else? Who will bring any charge against God's elect? It is God who justifies. Who is to condemn? It is Christ Jesus, who died, yes, who was raised, who is at the right hand of God, who indeed intercedes for us. Who will separate us from the love of Christ? Will hardship, or distress, or persecution, or famine, or nakedness, or peril, or sword? . . . No, in all these things we are more than conquerors through him who loved us. For I am convinced that neither death, nor life, nor angels, nor rulers, nor things present, nor things to come, nor powers, nor height, nor depth, nor anything else in all creation, will be able to separate us from the love of God in Christ Jesus our Lord.

Chapter 5

When You Feel Alone

Illness interrupts our life. The normal flow of life in family, work, and friendship changes. The routine around which we build our day is gone, and we find ourselves alone for long periods of time. Even when we are with others, there can be a sense of awkwardness, of not knowing what to say or keeping at a safe distance. The day stretches out before us like a desert and the night is foreboding.

But the isolation of illness can be an opportunity. If we can find some measure of acceptance of our aloneness, it can be a time to understand ourselves better and to seek more earnestly the presence of God. Jesus regularly sought to be alone and went out into the desert to pray. In the desert of our illness, let us turn to our loving God.

❧ A Brief Time of Prayer ❧

Psalm 73:22–28

Antiphon: You, O Lord, are the strength of my heart.

With you, I am always with you.
You hold me tight your hand in mine.
You will bring all things to a good end,
you lead me on, in your good pleasure.

What is heaven to me without you?
Where am I on earth if you are not there?
Though my body is broken down,
though my heart dies,
you are my rock, my God,
the future that waits for me.

Far away from you, life is not life.
To break faith with you, is to be no one.

With you, my highest good, my God,
with you I am secure.

For me it is good to be near God;
I have made the Lord God my refuge,
to tell of all your works.

Repeat Antiphon

Psalm Prayer

You are always with me, Lord, even when I feel all alone. Be a light in my darkness to preserve me from discouragement. Though my flesh and my heart may fail, you are my constant companion and my ever faithful friend.

Reading

John 15:14–17 *You are my friend.*

You are my friends if you do what I command you. I do not call you servants any longer, because the servant does not know what the master is doing; but I have called you friends, because I have made known to you everything that I have heard from my Father. You did not choose me but I chose you. And I appointed you to go and bear fruit, fruit that will last, so that the Father will give you whatever you ask him in my name. I am giving you these commands so that you may love one another.

Breath Prayer

Repeat this prayer in rhythm with your breathing for as long as you wish.

Abide in me, as I abide in you.

Closing Prayer

Pray the Our Father or one of the Canticles in the Everyday Prayers section of the book.

❧ Prayers for Coping With Loneliness ❧

Why Am I Lonely?

Lord, why do I feel so lonely?
It is not that no one cares about me,
or that no one visits me.
I have many friends.
They call, they visit, they send flowers.
Yet sometimes I feel all alone.

The presence of others soothes this pain,
but it is only a temporary relief.
Even when they are with me,
there is a loneliness that gnaws at me.
They don't understand what I am going through,
my pain, my fear, my uncertainty.

I should be able to handle this, but I can't.
I am afraid, Lord, to let others in.
They have their own burdens, they don't
    need mine.
They don't need to spend their time worrying
    about me.

Maybe they will think I am weak and whiney.
Maybe they'd rather not listen to me.

So many reasons to stay in my loneliness,
to hide in my fear.
Teach me, O Lord, how to let others in,
give me the courage to open my heart.
Let me know your love
so that I can trust others more.

When the Going Gets Tough

It's a time to be quiet
a time to rest,

I say to myself, Yes
that would be best:

It will all be well—
just wait it out,

and meanwhile, keep looking around and about
to see all the beauty that there is to see
created by God for one such as me.

But still a small voice inside me cries
Lord, grant that this time quickly flies—

for I'm finding today so very tough
and I honestly feel it's been long enough.

Calvary came just once for you
for me it begins each day anew.
And yes, I will keep looking around me to see
the beauty created for one such as me—

and hope—
that someday I will get up and go
out in the wind and the rain and the snow,
and not have the worry, the fear and the pain—

but lift up my face to the soft gentle rain—
and know that tomorrow I'll wake up and find
that this time of suffering is left far behind.
     —Aine Ni Maille

Prayer for Strength of Spirit

Sometimes, it's very hard to pray, God,
when I feel so absorbed in my pain
and in not knowing what all this means.
I can't help but ask why?
     Why me?
     Why now?
In searching for these answers,

I somehow feel you are near,
helping me to cope
with all the changes I experience.
Gentle God, help me to be patient.
Let me feel that in being sick
I am coming to know you better.
Let me care for me so that I may gain
strength of spirit once again.
   —Valerie Lesniak, C.S.J.

They Don't Call

They don't call.
They don't come.
I feel invisible, forgotten.
I know they are busy.
I've been busy myself.
But . . . it means so much.
Maybe they don't realize it,
as I didn't, back when . . .
But, right now,
I feel forgotten
by those I love most.
Empty, when I'd rather be full,
is how I come to You, this day, my God.
   —Marlene Halpin, O.P.

❧ Readings for Times of Loneliness ❧

In Communion With Jesus *Loneliness is one of the more painful aspects of illness. Yet we are never left alone.*

The essential mystery of the cross is that it gives rise to a certain kind of loneliness, an inability to see clearly how things are unfolding, an inability to see that, ultimately, all things will work together for our good, and that we are, indeed, not alone.

This sense of being abandoned, this extreme experience of loneliness, is evident in Jesus' cry: "My God, my God, why have you forsaken me?" (Mt. 27:46). If the Lord experienced pain and suffering, can we, his disciples, expect anything less? No! Like Jesus, we too must expect pain. There is, however, a decisive difference between our pain as disciples and that experienced by those who are *not* the Lord's disciples. The difference stems from that fact that, as disciples, we suffer in communion with the Lord. And that makes all the difference in the world. Nevertheless, even this communion does not totally extinguish the loneliness, the sense of abandonment, no more than it did for Jesus.

—Joseph Cardinal Bernardin

Mark 14:32–42 *"Stay with me." Jesus said these words to his disciples as he faced his death. He, too, knew loneliness.*

They went to a place called Gethsemane; and he said to his disciples, "Sit here while I pray." He took with him Peter and James and John, and began to be distressed and agitated. And he said to them, "I am deeply grieved, even to death; remain here, and keep awake." And going a little farther, he threw himself on the ground and prayed that, if it were possible, the hour might pass from him. He said, "Abba, Father, for you all things are possible; remove this cup from me; yet, not what I want, but what you want." He came and found them sleeping; and he said to Peter, "Simon, are you asleep? Could you not keep awake one hour? Keep awake and pray that you may not come into the time of trial; the spirit indeed is willing, but the flesh is weak." And again he went away and prayed, saying the same words. And once more he came and found them sleeping, for their eyes were very heavy; and they did not know what to say to him. He came a third time and said to them, "Are you still sleeping and taking your rest? Enough! The hour has come; the Son of Man is betrayed into the hands of sinners. Get up, let us be going. See, my betrayer is at hand."

Chapter 6

When You Are Facing Death

Death comes to all of us. To some it comes unexpectedly, suddenly. There is no time to prepare oneself, no opportunity to say goodbye, to heal old wounds, to comfort and strengthen loved ones. But for you, there is this time, this opportunity.

As Jesus approached his last days, he gathered his disciples around him. He spoke lovingly to them, he washed their feet, he gave them the eucharist as the sacrament of his eternal presence. Let Jesus guide you in these days to know what to say and what to do. Let him strengthen you to overcome your fear and to share your love for others, for love is stronger than death.

❧ A Brief Time of Prayer ❧

Psalm 23

Antiphon: Though I walk through the valley of death, I shall not fear.

The LORD is my shepherd,
I shall not want.
He makes me lie down in green pastures;
he leads me beside still waters;
he restores my soul.
He leads me in right paths for his name's sake.

Even though I walk through the darkest valley,
I fear no evil;
for you are with me;
your rod and your staff—
they comfort me.

You prepare a table before me
in the presence of my enemies;
you anoint my head with oil;
my cup overflows.
Surely goodness and mercy shall follow me
all the days of my life,

and I shall dwell in the house of the LORD
my whole life long.

Repeat Antiphon

Psalm Prayer

Jesus, gentle shepherd, you have been with me all
the days of my life. Be with me now as I walk
through the valley of death. Forgive all my sins,
and lead me safely home. I place my trust in you.

Reading

John 14:1–3 *"I have prepared a place for you."*

"Do not let your hearts be troubled. Believe in
God, believe also in me. In my Father's house there
are many dwelling places. If it were not so, would
I have told you that I go to prepare a place for you?
And if I go and prepare a place for you, I will come
again and will take you to myself, so that where I
am, there you may be also."

Breath Prayer

Repeat this prayer in rhythm with your breathing for as long as you wish.

The Lord is my shepherd.

Closing Prayer

Pray the Our Father or one of the Canticles in the Everyday Prayers section of the book.

✎ Prayers When Death Is Near ✎

At the Hour of My Death

O God, give me of thy wisdom,
O God, give me of thy mercy,
O God, give me of thy fullness,
  and of thy guidance in the face of every strait.
O God, give me of thy holiness,
O God, give me of thy shielding,
O God, give me of thy surrounding,
  and of the peace in the knot of my death.
O give me of thy surrounding,
  and of thy peace at the hour of my death.
  —*Carmina Gaedelica*

Into Your Hands, O God

This solitude,
Into your hands, O God,
This emptiness,
Into your hands, O God,
This loneliness,
Into your hands—
This all.
Into your hands, O God,

This grief,
Into your hands, O God—
What is left,
What is left
Of me.
  —Edwina Gateley

Great Distress

O Lord God,
Great distress has come upon me;
My cares threaten to crush me,
And I do not know what to do.
O God, be gracious to me and help me.
Give me strength to bear what you send,

And do not let fear rule over me;
Take a father's care of my wife and children.

O merciful God,
Forgive me all the sins that I have committed
Against you and against my fellow men.
I trust in your grace
and commit my life wholly into your hands.
Do with me according to your will
And as is best for me.

Whether I live or die, I am with you,
And you, my God are with me.
Lord, I wait for your salvation
And for your kingdom. Amen.
    —Dietrich Bonhoeffer

Anima Christi

Soul of Christ, sanctify me.
Body of Christ, save me.
Blood of Christ, inebriate me.
Water from the side of Christ, wash me.
Passion of Christ, strengthen me.
O good Jesus, hear me.
Permit me not to be separated from you.
From the wicked foe defend me.
And bid me come to you
That with your saints I may praise you
Forever and ever.
    —Ignatius of Loyola

Prayer of Abandonment

Father,
I abandon myself into your hands;
do with me what you will.

Whatever you may do, I thank you:
I am ready for all, I accept all.
Let only your will be done in me,
and in all your creatures—
I wish no more than this, O Lord.
Into your hands I commend my soul;
I offer it to you with all the love of my Heart,
For I love you, Lord, and so need to give myself,
to surrender myself into your hands
    without reserve,
and with boundless confidence,
for you are my Father.
    —Charles de Foucauld

❧ Readings When Death Is Near ❧

Life-Changing Knowledge *The knowledge of your coming death is an opportunity to use the time ahead well.*

Not everyone gets to know ahead of time what
  you now know.
Death, for many, is a surprise—a sneaky,
  stealthy thief
  striking without warning,
  like that sad September morning.
You know that you are dying. . . .
You've been tipped off
  So what will you do with the warning?
A diagnosis can be turned into good,
  life-changing knowledge.
A diagnosis can be turned into time to listen,
  time to hear;
  time to finish up, time to resolve;
  time to get around to doing what you haven't
    gotten around to;
  time to ask questions and ponder answers;

time to wrestle with the mysteries and the
   unexplainables;
time to be strong, time to be weak;
time to confront fears, time to shed tears, and
   time to get your affairs in order.
Most importantly it becomes a time to make
choices
   to die while living well. To die well.
   —Harold Ivan Smith

Matthew 11:28–30 *Jesus invites us to find comfort in him.*

"Come to me, all you that are weary and are carrying heavy burdens, and I will give you rest. Take my yoke upon you, and learn from me; for I am gentle and humble in heart, and you will find rest for your souls. For my yoke is easy, and my burden is light."

Chapter 7

When You Seek Forgiveness

Illness doesn't leave us much middle ground. While it often brings out the best in us, sometimes it brings out the worst. Caught up in our own pain, we can sometimes hurt others. Sickness makes everybody vulnerable and it can be irresistibly easy to strike out at others when we are hurting.

Sometimes the isolation and suffering of sickness can force us to see ourselves more clearly; it reveals things about us that need to be changed.

Take heart in the words of Jesus, who said that he came not for the righteous, but for sinners. Ask for his forgiveness and healing, for he knows us and loves us despite our sins.

❦ A Brief Time of Prayer ❧

Psalm 51:1–13

Antiphon: Create in me a clean heart, O God.

Have mercy on me, O God,
according to your steadfast love;
according to your abundant mercy
blot out my transgressions.
Wash me thoroughly from my iniquity,
and cleanse me from my sin.

For I know my transgressions,
and my sin is ever before me.
Against you, you alone, have I sinned,
and done what is evil in your sight,
so that you are justified in your sentence
and blameless when you pass judgment.

Indeed, I was born guilty,
a sinner when my mother conceived me.
You desire truth in the inward being;
therefore teach me wisdom in my secret heart.
Purge me with hyssop, and I shall be clean;

wash me, and I shall be whiter than snow.
Let me hear joy and gladness;

let the bones that you have crushed rejoice.
Hide your face from my sins,
and blot out all my iniquities.

Create in me a clean heart, O God,
and put a new and right spirit within me.
Do not cast me away from your presence,
and do not take your holy spirit from me.

Restore to me the joy of your salvation,
and sustain in me a willing spirit.
Then I will teach transgressors your ways,
and sinners will return to you.

Repeat Antiphon

Psalm Prayer

Loving Father, your mercy is abundant and your love is steadfast. I ask your forgiveness for all my sins. Create a clean heart in me and cleanse me from every desire that does not lead to you. Send me your Holy Spirit to keep me ever close to your son Jesus.

Reading

Luke 15:1–7 *The Good Shepherd seeks us out.*

Now all the tax collectors and sinners were coming near to listen to him. And the Pharisees and the scribes were grumbling and saying, "This fellow welcomes sinners and eats with them." So he told them this parable: "Which one of you, having a hundred sheep and losing one of them, does not leave the ninety-nine in the wilderness and go after the one that is lost until he finds it? When he has found it, he lays it on his shoulders and rejoices. And when he comes home, he calls together his friends and neighbors, saying to them, 'Rejoice with me, for I have found my sheep that was lost.' Just so, I tell you, there will be more joy in heaven over one sinner who repents than over ninety-nine righteous persons who need no repentance."

Breath Prayer

Repeat this prayer in rhythm with your breathing for as long as you wish.

Jesus, Son of the living God, have mercy on me, a sinner.

Closing Prayer

Pray the Our Father or one of the Canticles in the Everyday Prayers section of the book.

❧ Prayers for Forgiveness ❧

Jesus, Gentle Shepherd

Jesus, gentle shepherd,
look with mercy on me,
for even in my illness
I have wandered away from you,
    and I need your mercy and forgiveness.
Forgive my harsh words,
my ungrateful silences,
my resentful thoughts,
my angry complaints,
my self-centered moodiness.
For I know, O Lord,
that my sins hurt those who care for me,
and close me to the gift of your presence.
Open my heart, my mind, my whole body
to the grace of your forgiveness and healing.
I give you thanks, O Lord,
for your presence with me this day.

For a Change of Heart

I am lost, O God,
and I cannot find the way.
I do not know if you hear me,
or if you will respond,
but still I cry out to you
to save me from myself.

I don't know who I am anymore,
my certainties are all gone.
My body is miserable,
my spirit is despondent.
My foundations are crumbling,
all the while the storm batters me.

I have been ungrateful, self-centered, hurtful.
But still I cry out to you:
hear me, help me, heal me.
Let me begin again,
even in the midst of this sickness.
Give me strength to start anew.

You who came to call sinners,
hear my poor prayer.

O Heart of Love

O Heart of Love,
I put all my trust in you.
For I fear all things
   that spring from my own weakness,
but I hope for all things
   that come from your goodness.
   —Margaret Mary Alacoque

☙ Readings About Forgiveness ❧

Like Summer Seas *Let us be grateful for God's gentle and faithful way.*

Like summer seas that lave with silent tides a lonely shore, like whispering winds that stir the tops of forest trees, like a still small voice that calls to us in the watches of the night, like a child's hand that feels about a fast closed door, gentle, unnoticed, and oft in vain; so is thy coming unto us, O God.

Like ships storm-driven into port, like starving souls that seek the bread they once despised, like wanderers begging refuge from the whelming night, like prodigals that seek the father's home when all is spent; yet welcomed at the open door, arms outstretched and kisses for our shame; so is our coming unto thee, O God.

Like flowers uplifted to the sun, like trees that bend before the storm, like sleeping seas that mirror cloudless skies, like a harp to the hand, like an echo to a cry, like a song to the heart; for all our stubbornness, our failure, and our sin; so would we have been to thee, O God.
—W. E. Orchard

Luke 7:36–50 *Jesus forgives the sinful woman at Simon's house.*

One of the Pharisees asked Jesus to eat with him, and he went into the Pharisee's house and took his place at the table. And a woman in the city, who was a sinner, having learned that he was eating in the Pharisee's house, brought an alabaster jar of ointment. She stood behind him at his feet, weeping, and began to bathe his feet with her tears and to dry them with her hair. Then she continued kissing his feet and anointing them with the ointment.

Now when the Pharisee who had invited him saw it, he said to himself, "If this man were a prophet, he would have known who and what kind of woman this is who is touching him—that she is a sinner."

Jesus spoke up and said to him, "Simon, I have something to say to you." "Teacher," he replied, "Speak." "A certain creditor had two debtors; one owed five hundred denarii, and the other fifty. When they could not pay, he canceled the debts for both of them. Now which of them will love him more?"

Simon answered, "I suppose the one for whom he canceled the greater debt." And Jesus said to him, "You have judged rightly." Then turning toward the woman, he said to Simon, "Do you see this woman? I entered your house; you gave me no water for my feet, but she has bathed my feet with her tears and dried them with her hair. You gave me no kiss, but from the time I came in she has not stopped kissing my feet. You did not anoint my head with oil, but she has anointed my feet with ointment. Therefore, I tell you, her sins, which were many, have been forgiven; hence she has shown great love. But the one to whom little is forgiven, loves little."

Then he said to her, "Your sins are forgiven." But those who were at the table with him began to say among themselves, "Who is this who even forgives sins?" And he said to the woman, "Your faith has saved you; go in peace."

Chapter 8

When You Want to Pray for Others

Illness gives us a sense of solidarity with the pain and suffering of others. And it teaches us to be grateful for each act of kindness, each expression of care. Sometimes it's hard to be in a position of constantly receiving from others. We feel helpless to give back.

But one thing we can do is pray for others, for those who care for us and for others who may be suffering, perhaps more than us. And as we pray, because we pray, others may sense a peace in us, an openness, a presence of God that is an invitation to them. This is what we can give.

❧ A Brief Time of Prayer ❧

Psalm 34:1–10

Antiphon: I give you thanks, O Lord, for the ways you care for me.

I will bless the LORD at all times;
his praise shall continually be in my mouth.
My soul makes its boast in the LORD;
let the humble hear and be glad.

O magnify the LORD with me,
and let us exalt his name together.
I sought the LORD, and he answered me,
and delivered me from all my fears.

Look to him, and be radiant;
so your faces shall never be ashamed.
This poor soul cried, and was heard by the LORD,
and was saved from every trouble.

The angel of the LORD encamps
around those who fear him, and delivers them.
O taste and see that the LORD is good;
happy are those who take refuge in him.

O fear the LORD, you his holy ones,
for those who fear him have no want.
The young lions suffer want and hunger,
but those who seek the LORD lack no good thing.

Repeat Antiphon

Psalm Prayer

Compassionate God, I bless and praise you for
your constant love and care in my life. Thank you
for all those who love and care for me in this time
of illness; be with them in their needs as you have
been with me in mine. May we together always
give you praise and thanks.

Reading

Mark 2:1–12 *We come to Jesus with the help of others.*

When he returned to Capernaum after some days,
it was reported that he was at home. So many
gathered around that there was no longer room for
them, not even in front of the door; and he was
speaking the word to them. Then some people
came, bringing to him a paralyzed man, carried by
four of them. And when they could not bring him
to Jesus because of the crowd, they removed the
roof above him; and after having dug through it,
they let down the mat on which the paralytic lay.
When Jesus saw their faith, he said to the paralytic,

"Son, your sins are forgiven." Now some of the scribes were sitting there, questioning in their hearts, "Why does this fellow speak in this way? It is blasphemy! Who can forgive sins but God alone?" At once Jesus perceived in his spirit that they were discussing these questions among themselves; and he said to them, "Why do you raise such questions in your hearts? Which is easier, to say to the paralytic, 'Your sins are forgiven,' or to say, 'Stand up and take your mat and walk'? But so that you may know that the Son of Man has authority on earth to forgive sins"—he said to the paralytic—"I say to you, stand up, take your mat and go to your home." And he stood up, and immediately took the mat and went out before all of them; so that they were all amazed and glorified God, saying, "We have never seen anything like this!"

Breath Prayer

Repeat this prayer in rhythm with your breathing for as long as you wish.

Keep us, O Lord, always in your love.

Closing Prayer

Pray the Our Father or one of the Canticles in the Everyday Prayers section of the book.

❧ Prayers for Others ❧

For My Family

Loving God, thank you for the gift of my family and for all the ways they have shown their love and concern for me. My illness is difficult for them too—it is draining, it is worrisome. Be with them to strengthen them when they are weary or discouraged. Ease their burdens, calm their fears, heal their wounds. Lord, you have brought us together and made us a family, teach us how to grow closer at this time and give us your guidance in the days ahead.

For Others Who Are Sick

Lord, help me to remember that I am not alone in my illness. There are others in my family, in my circle of friends and acquaintances, and here in this hospital in need of your healing love.

Pause and mention any family members by name.

Accept my prayer, O Lord, and join it with theirs, be it spoken aloud, whispered in their hearts, or struggling to find expression. Help me not to get so caught up in myself that I forget about their needs, their pain, their worries. Lord, we are one in our need for you, may our prayers too be united, so we may call out to you in one voice.

For My Caregivers

In this time of illness, Lord, you have sent so many people to care for me—not only family and friends, but strangers who have been so kind and generous. Thank you for their many and varied gifts; may each one find the strength, the compassion, and the wisdom to continue to care for others.

Take a moment to name particular caregivers and pray for their needs.

Lord, you have placed in each of them the desire to care and the gifts to heal. Be at their sides as they do your work and send them the comfort of your Spirit to renew their strength.

Readings

Good Friends *In illness, we are especially grateful for the love of others. But you also have a gift to give them.*

The friends who have supported us best are those who in their distinctive way have made it clear that they love us. It is impossible to have too many people telling you persuasively . . . that they love you.

Sick people of any sensitivity soon find that they have to let themselves be cared for, worried over, exalted beyond their merits—in a word, loved. That is part of the job description of being sick, especially of being sick terminally. Your fate reminds all who see you that they are also mortal. Your fate becomes a nutshell in which the pathos of the entire human condition rests. . . .

No matter how healthy they are now, most of the friends who come to visit will eventually be more like you than different. Whatever you can do to make trust in God, agreement to what God makes happen, seem natural and easy will be a blessing.

—John Carmody

Philippians 1:3–11 *We hold each other in our hearts.*

I thank my God every time I remember you, constantly praying with joy in every one of my prayers for all of you, because of your sharing in the gospel from the first day until now. I am confident of this, that the one who began a good work among you will bring it to completion by the day of Jesus Christ. It is right for me to think this way about all of you, because you hold me in your heart, for all of you share in God's grace with me, both in my imprisonment and in the defense and confirmation of the gospel. For God is my witness, how I long for all of you with the compassion of Christ Jesus. And this is my prayer, that your love may overflow more and more with knowledge and full insight to help you to determine what is best, so that in the day of Christ you may be pure and blameless, having produced the harvest of righteousness that comes through Jesus Christ for the glory and praise of God.

Chapter 9

When You Are Grateful

When we are ill, we recognize what really matters. And we recognize how much we have to be grateful for. We stop taking things for granted. It can be a humbling experience, but hopefully it has a lasting effect on us.

When the illusion of our independence is shattered and we learn to accept our dependence on others and on God, we realize that everything in our life is a gift. We realize how good God is, and how much we have been blessed. "Thank you, Lord" becomes our most heartfelt prayer.

☙ A Brief Time of Prayer ❧

Psalm 138

Antiphon: In your love you never forsake me.

I give you thanks, O LORD, with my whole heart;
before the gods I sing your praise;
I bow down toward your holy temple
and give thanks to your name
for your steadfast love and your faithfulness;
for you have exalted your name
and your word above everything.

On the day I called, you answered me,
you increased my strength of soul.
All the kings of the earth shall praise you,
   O LORD,
for they have heard the words of your mouth.
They shall sing of the ways of the LORD,
for great is the glory of the LORD.

For though the LORD is high, he regards the lowly;
but the haughty he perceives from far away.
Though I walk in the midst of trouble,

you preserve me against the wrath of my enemies;
you stretch out your hand,
and your right hand delivers me.

The LORD will fulfill his purpose for me;
your steadfast love, O LORD, endures forever.
Do not forsake the work of your hands.

Repeat Antiphon

Psalm Prayer

I give you thanks, O Lord, with all my heart for all your gifts to me. Your love endures through all things, and though I am in distress, you never leave me alone. Help me to trust you more and more, and in all circumstances to give you thanks.

Reading

Luke 17:11–19 *Remember God's goodness and give thanks.*

On the way to Jerusalem Jesus was going through the region between Samaria and Galilee. As he entered a village, ten lepers approached him. Keeping their distance, they called out, saying, "Jesus, Master, have mercy on us!" When he saw them, he said to them, "Go and show yourselves to the priests." And as they went, they were made clean. Then one of them, when he saw that he was healed, turned back, praising God with a loud voice. He prostrated himself at Jesus' feet and thanked him. And he was a Samaritan. Then Jesus asked, "Were not ten made clean? But the other nine, where are they? Was none of them found to return and give praise to God except this foreigner?" Then he said to him, "Get up and go on your way; your faith has made you well."

Breath Prayer

Repeat this prayer in rhythm with your breathing for as long as you wish.

From the depths of my heart, I give you thanks.

Closing Prayer

Pray the Our Father or one of the Canticles in the Everyday Prayers section of the book.

❧ Prayers of Gratitude ❧

A Living Sacrifice

Teach me, Lord God,
to offer my body as a living sacrifice to you:
my head, my arms, my legs;
my conscious and my unconscious—
impulses, thoughts, desires, ambitions—
all the known and unknown
that make up the real me.
Teach me, also,
to offer those parts of my body
which are sick and disabled.
Cleanse me, heal me,
and renew me by your Spirit.
Through the offering of your beloved Son
on the cross of Calvary,
may the offering of my body
be a spiritual act of worship
holy and pleasing to you.
   —John Gunstone

Day by Day

Thank you Lord Jesus Christ,
for all the benefits and blessings
which you have given to me,
for all the pains and insults
which you have borne for me.
Merciful Friend, Brother, and Redeemer,
let me know you more clearly,
love you more dearly,
and follow you more nearly,
day by day.
   —St. Richard of Chichester

Gratitude for Caregivers

Thank you, God, for all the people you have provided to take care of me in this time of illness. Thank you for the knowledge and wisdom they have worked so hard to acquire, for the gentle care and concern they show even when their tasks are unpleasant, and for the patience and compassion they offer when I am most in need. Help me to recognize you in them, and may I in turn be a sign of your presence by my gratitude for their service.

❧ Readings for Times of Gratitude ❧

The Power of Appreciation *The conscious practice of gratitude offers us both peace and healing.*

People wonder if there are tried and true ways to overcome the strains and tensions they feel between themselves and their surroundings. They ask, "How can we regain joy and serenity in our life?" Our answer to this oft-repeated question is based on the conviction that appreciation is the single most important disposition in the world today. The power of appreciation helps us look at the directions for living offered by everyday events, good, bad, and indifferent, in a new way. . . .

How do we make sense out of the events that shape our day-to-day existence? How can we develop an outlook that will help us to find lasting meaning in life? One answer is to redirect your feelings, thoughts, and decisions in a way that stimulates appreciation. You may soon discover that life, with all its ups and downs, may challenge and surprise you, but never defeat you.

—Adrian van Kaam and Susan Muto

Philippians 4:4–7 *Rejoice always and give thanks.*

Rejoice in the Lord always; again I will say, Rejoice. Let your gentleness be known to everyone. The Lord is near. Do not worry about anything, but in everything by prayer and supplication with thanksgiving let your requests be made known to God. And the peace of God, which surpasses all understanding, will guard your hearts and your minds in Christ Jesus.

Chapter 10

When You Want to Deepen Your Trust

Illness shakes our foundation. It forces us to take stock, to assess whether we've built the house of our lives on shifting sands or on firm rock. Most likely, some of our foundation is just fine, while other parts are a bit weak and need shoring up.

Illness can be an opportunity to discover where in our lives we need to place more of our trust in God. Reflect on your priorities, on the quality of your relationships, on your care for yourself, and on the place of God in your life. Ask God to help you live a life of trust in his care.

❧ A Brief Time of Prayer ❧

Psalm 62:1–2, 5–8, 11–12

Antiphon: All my hope is in you, O Lord.

For God alone my soul waits in silence;
from him comes my salvation.
He alone is my rock and my salvation,
   my fortress;
I shall never be shaken.

For God alone my soul waits in silence,
for my hope is from him.
He alone is my rock and my salvation,
   my fortress;
I shall not be shaken.

On God rests my deliverance and my honor;
my mighty rock, my refuge is in God.
Trust in him at all times, O people;
pour out your heart before him; God is a refuge
   for us.

Once God has spoken; twice have I heard this:
that power belongs to God,
and steadfast love belongs to you, O Lord.
For you repay to all according to their work.

Repeat Antiphon

Psalm Prayer

For you alone I wait, O Lord. In silence, in
stillness, in the darkness of night. You are my
rock, my refuge, my fortress. Teach me, O Lord, to
pour out my soul to you and to trust you in all
things. Amen.

Reading

John 20:24–29 *I believe Lord, help my unbelief.*

But Thomas (who was called the Twin), one of the
twelve, was not with them when Jesus came. So
the other disciples told him, "We have seen the
Lord." But he said to them, "Unless I see the mark
of the nails in his hands, and put my finger in the
mark of the nails and my hand in his side, I will not
believe." A week later his disciples were again in
the house, and Thomas was with them. Although
the doors were shut, Jesus came and stood among
them and said, "Peace be with you." Then he said

to Thomas, "Put your finger here and see my hands. Reach out your hand and put it in my side. Do not doubt but believe." Thomas answered him, "My Lord and my God!" Jesus said to him, "Have you believed because you have seen me? Blessed are those who have not seen and yet have come to believe."

Breath Prayer

Repeat this prayer in rhythm with your breathing for as long as you wish.

Jesus, my Lord, Jesus, my God.

Closing Prayer

Pray the Our Father or one of the Canticles in the Everyday Prayers section of the book.

❧ Prayers to Deepen Our Trust ❧

Prayer of Dedication

Lord, I freely yield all my freedom to you.
Take my memory, my intellect, and my
    entire will.
You have given me anything I am or have;
I give it all back to you to stand under your
    will alone.
Your love and your grace are enough for me;
I shall ask for nothing more.
    —St. Ignatius of Loyola

You Have Walked This Path

Lord Jesus,
thank you for walking this path ahead of me,
and for showing me the way through suffering
by your patience and acceptance,
    and by your selfless gift of your very life.
Help me to hold on to you,
and not to run from my dependence on others.
Do not let me forget what really matters,
let me take nothing for granted,
and recognize all that I have to be grateful for.

❧ Readings to Deepen Our Trust ❧

The Book of Our Lives *Our lives are a story that the Spirit of God is writing.*

The Holy Spirit writes no more gospels except in our hearts. All we do from moment to moment is live this new gospel. We are the paper; our sufferings and actions are the ink. The workings of the Holy Spirit are the pen, and with it he writes a living gospel; but it will never be read till that last day of glory when it leaves the printing press of this life.

And what a splendid book it will be—the book the Holy Spirit is still writing! The book is on press, and never a day passes when the type is not set, ink applied and pages pulled. But we remain in the light of faith. The paper is blacker than the ink, and the paper is pied; the language is not of this world and we understand nothing. We shall be able to read it only in heaven.

—Jean-Pierre de Caussade

Luke 1:26–38 *Let it be with me according to your word.*

In the sixth month the angel Gabriel was sent by God to a town in Galilee called Nazareth, to a virgin engaged to a man whose name was Joseph, of the house of David. The virgin's name was Mary. And he came to her and said, "Greetings, favored one! The Lord is with you."

But she was much perplexed by his words and pondered what sort of greeting this might be. The angel said to her, "Do not be afraid, Mary, for you have found favor with God. And now, you will conceive in your womb and bear a son, and you will name him Jesus. He will be great, and will be called the Son of the Most High, and the Lord God will give to him the throne of his ancestor David. He will reign over the house of Jacob forever, and of his kingdom there will be no end."

Mary said to the angel, "How can this be, since I am a virgin?" The angel said to her, "The Holy Spirit will come upon you, and the power of the Most High will overshadow you; therefore the child to be born will be holy; he will be called Son of God. And now, your relative Elizabeth in her old age has also conceived a son; and this is the sixth month for her who was said to be barren. For nothing will be impossible with God."

Then Mary said, "Here am I, the servant of the Lord; let it be with me according to your word." Then the angel departed from her.

Index of Prayers

Acknowledgments

Unattributed works are by the author. A brief description of lesser known writers, whose prayers are in the public domain, is provided.

Readings

"The Book of Our Lives" by Jean-Pierre de Caussade is excerpted from *Abandonment to Divine Providence*, New York: Doubleday & Co., 1975. De Caussade was an eighteenth-century French Jesuit.

"The Cup of Suffering" by Henri Nouwen is excerpted from *Can You Drink the Cup?* Notre Dame, IN: Ave Maria Press, 1996. Used by permission.

"Fear Not" by William Barry is excerpted from "The Kingdom of God and Discernment," *America*, Vol. 157, No. 7 (September 26, 1987), p. 159.

"Good Friends" by John Carmody is excerpted from *Cancer and Faith: Reflections on Living With a Terminal Illness*, Mystic, CT: Twenty-Third Publications, 1994, pp. 68–69.

"In Communion With Jesus" by Joseph Cardinal Bernardin is excerpted from *The Gift of Peace: Personal Reflections*, Chicago: Loyola Press, 1997.

"Life-Changing Knowledge" by Harold Ivan Smith is excerpted from *Finding Your Way When Death Is Near*, Notre Dame, IN: Ave Maria Press, 2002, pp. 11–15.

"Like Summer Seas" by W. E. Orchard is excerpted from *The Temple*, New York: E.P. Dutton & Co., Inc., 1918, p. 149. Found in *Comfort Ye My People: A Manual for Pastoral Ministry*, Russell B. Dicks, New York: The Macmillan Company, 1947.

"The Power of Appreciation" by Adrian van Kaam and Susan Muto is excerpted from *The Power of Appreciation*, New York: Crossroad Publishing, 1993, pp. 19, 21.

"Where Is God?" by C. S. Lewis is excerpted from *Morning and Evening Prayer with Selected Psalms and Readings for the Church Year*, compiled and edited by Howard Galley, New York: Church Hymnal Corp., 1994.

"Why Me?" by Wayne Muller is excerpted from *Legacy of the Heart*, New York: Simon & Schuster, 1992.

Prayers

"Anima Christi" and "Prayer of Dedication," St. Ignatius of Loyola.

"O Living Christ" by Russell B. Dicks is excerpted from *Comfort Ye My People: A Manual for Pastoral Ministry*, New York: The Macmillan Company, 1947.

"The Power of Cancer" by Gregory Smutko, O.F.M. Cap. is used by permission of the author.

"Prayer for Strength of Spirit" by Valerie Lesniak, C.S.J. is used by permission of St. Joseph Regional Medical Center, South Bend, IN.

"Psalm 73" by Huub Oosterhuis, et al., is excerpted from *Fifty Psalms: An Attempt at a New Translation*, New York: Herder and Herder, 1969.

"They Don't Call" by Marlene Halpin is excerpted from *Right Side Up! Reflections for Those Living With Serious Illness*, Dubuque, IA: Islewest Publishing, 1995. Used by permission of the author.

"When the Going Gets Tough" by Aine Ni Maille is used by permission of the author..

"Where There Is Pain" by John D. Powers is excerpted from *Fear Not, I Am With You.* Staten Island, NY: Alba House, 1990.

"You Know What Pain Is Like" by William Barclay is excerpted from *Fear Not, I Am With You*, Staten Island, NY: Alba House, 1990. Used by permission.